ANNE FRANK
THE DIARY OF A YOUNG GIRL

by
Anne Frank

D1560956

Student Packet

Written by
Phyllis A. Green

Contains masters for:

1	Anticipation Activity
5	Vocabulary Activities
1	Study Guide (six pages)
1	Character Analysis
1	Decision-Making
1	Puzzle on Diary Writing Format
1	Character Analysis / Higher Order Thinking
1	Character Analysis / Synthesis
5	Writing Activities
1	Comprehension Quiz — After Page 79
1	Comprehension Quiz — Pages 80-174
1	Final Examination

PLUS Detailed Answer Key

Note

The text used to prepare this guide was the Pocket Books paperback edition. The page references may differ in the hardcover or other paperback editions.

Please note: Please assess the appropriateness of this book for the age level and maturity of your students prior to reading and discussing it with your class.

ISBN 1-56137-607-8

To order, contact your local school supply store, or—

Novel Units, Inc.
P.O. Box 791610
San Antonio, TX 78279

Web site: www.educyberstor.com

Name_____

The Situation

You are thirteen and must go into hiding with your family and four other acquaintances. The authorities threaten all of you and a dangerous war is being waged around you outside. What are your questions and problems as you go into hiding? How do you prepare for your survival? With a partner select four problems you expect and put them into a question format. Exchange with another pair who will write answers to speculate on how you or Anne will handle the problems. After reading, answer the problems as Anne does.

My Problems in Question Form	Predicted Solutions	The Book's Solutions
1.		
2.		
3.		
4.		
5.		

Vocabulary

Directions: This listing of words is from pages 1-79 of *Anne Frank: The Diary of a Young Girl*. Read through the list, marking a check (√) if you positively know the word and a star (*) if you've seen the word before. Then, from context devise a definition for the words.

Word	Page	"Your Mark"	Definition
unbosomings	2		
pogroms	3		
speculations	5		
superfluous	11		
obstinate	24		
surreptitiously	27		
seclusion	32		
quicksilver	33		
Gestapo	34		
rendezvous	45		
lorries	48		
camomile	53		
venom	59		
procured	61		
haricot beans	63		
eucalyptus	67		
duodenal ulcer	75		
clandestine	75		
barrage	77		
het	78		
pedantic	79		

Name_____

Directions: For each of these word banks, read through the words, circling those you know, and placing a check by those you recognize but aren't absolutely sure. On the back of this sheet, note the checked words and unknown words. Write a brief definition and with a partner, devise a way to remember the word.

Before Page 80

tumult (page 81)	irrevocable (page 90)	consolation (page 105)
dispersed (page 82)	incessantly (page 93)	cremated (page 105)
coquetry (page 84)	capitulated (page 97)	lozenges (page 109)
supple (page 85)	grouses (page 100)	compresses (page 109)
eiderdown (page 86)	palpitations (page 103)	

Before Page 114

aggravating (page 115)	genealogical (page 129)	kale (page 156)
fortnight (page 122)	impudent (page 132)	hemorrhage (page 158)
diligently (page 122)	rummaging (page 137)	incessantly (page 159)
suffice (page 124)	scoffingly (page 150)	sallies (page 167)
sauntered (page 128)	coquettish (page 151)	stupendous (page 169)

Vocabulary Alert

Directions: Look over this list of words. Be sure you know them. Choose three to use in a sentence.

endive (page 175)	concentration camps (page 209)	redoubt (page 223)
kohlrabi (page 175)	coherent (page 209)	scudding (page 226)
beetroot (page 176)	capping (page 211)	supercilious (page 241)
impudence (page 180)	incalculable (page 213)	indignation (page 245)
reproached (page 186)	loathed (page 213)	totalitarian (page 247)
livid (page 189)	explicitly (page 214)	foreboding (page 248)
pseudonym (page 193)	asylum (page 215)	acquiesced (page 248)
jocular (page 196)	discord (page 215)	appeasement (page 249)
piccalilli (page 200)	abyss (page 216)	deportation (page 252)
clandestine (page 204)	dregs (page 216)	crematories (page 254)
teetotaler (page 206)	capitulation (page 219)	emaciated (page 255)

Sentences:

-

-

-

Analogies

Directions: Analogies express the relationships between words. They can be compared to certain mathematical equalities or equations (e.g., $1/2 = 2/4 = 3/6 = 4/8$).

In an analogy test question, you are asked to determine the relationship between a pair of words and then recognize a similar or parallel relationship between a different pair of words. Some of the more common word relationships displayed in analogies are the following:

part : whole	cause : effect	opposites	result
purpose	association	characteristic	place : person
degree	action : situation		

Choose among the words from the book in creating your own analogies.

Exchange with a partner to explain and defend your analogy.

My first analogy:

My second analogy:

My third analogy:

My fourth analogy:

Vocabulary Activity — More Analogies

Directions: Look for other common analogy types. Fill in the third column. Use the identified vocabulary words for extra credit.

Analogy	Example	My Example
definition	refuge : shelter	
defining characteristic	tiger : carnivorous	
class and member	sonnet : poem	
tool and its action	saw : cut	
time sequence	first : last	
gender	doe : stag	
age	colt : stallion	
worker and action	financier : invest	
tool and object it acts upon	knife : bread	

Study Guide

Directions: These questions are provided to assist the reader to understand the literal details of the book. A few opinion questions are also included. Your teacher will direct you in responding to the questions:

1. Write out short answers.

2. Be prepared to answer orally.

3. Make notes to enable small group discussion.

4. Preview the questions prior to reading a section.

Introductory Pages

1. What is the publishing history of the book?

2. Choose three significant words or phrases from the Preface and Introduction.

Pages 1-56 — Sunday, 14 June, 1942 to Tuesday, 22 December, 1942

1. How is the book arranged?

2. Complete these parts of a story map to explain the story:

   a) Setting—Where and when does the story take place?
   b) What is the conflict in the story?
   c) Who are the characters?

9

3.   What is the relationship between Anne and her diary, Kitty?

4.   Choose three incidents from this section to explain the mood in the Secret Annexe.

5.   What is the morality of the situation in 1942 in Holland?

Pages 57-79 — Wednesday, 13 January, 1943 to Tuesday, 13 July, 1943

1.   Fill in attribute webs for these themes in Anne's writing.

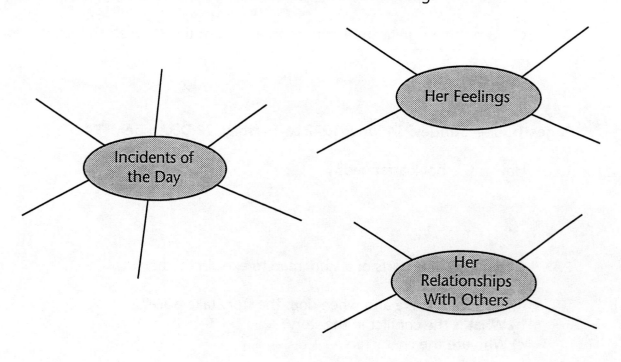

2.   How does the reading thus far make you feel?

Pages 80-114 — Friday, 16 July, 1943 to Wednesday, 29 December, 1943

1.   How does the second year in hiding differ from the first?

2.   What risks are there to those who provide food and help to the Secret Annexe residents?

3.   What dangers from the outside alarm the Secret Annexe folks from July to December, 1943?

4.   What dangers from the inside concern the Secret Annexe folks from July to December, 1943?

Pages 114-174 — Sunday, 2 January, 1944 to Friday, 31 March, 1944

1.   How does Anne's relationship with her mother, Margot, and Peter develop in this period?

11

2.   What happens in the war during early 1944?

3.   What is Anne's greatest wish in early 1944?

4.   How has Anne changed and developed since the beginning of the book?

Pages 174-205 — Saturday, 1 April 1944 to Sunday morning, 7 May, 1944

1.   What are Anne's aspirations for her future? Why are her aspirations appropriate?

2.   What happens on Good Friday, 1944?

3.   What are the unique strains for the Annexers while waiting for an explanation and resolution of the Easter weekend incident?

4.   What causes the strain between Anne and her parents in April, 1944?

5.   Why is Kraler livid with the Annexers in April, 1944? Is he justified? How do the Annexers react?

Pages 205-241 — Monday, 8 May, 1944 to Tuesday, 1 August, 1944

1. Find examples of the following emotions and feelings in this section of Anne's diary:

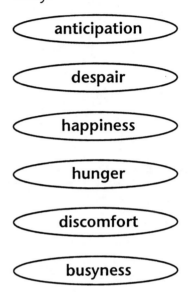

anticipation

despair

happiness

hunger

discomfort

busyness

2. What significant event of World War II occurs in this time period? How does it effect those in the Annexe?

3. What does Anne's statement, "A quiet conscience makes one strong" mean? (Thursday, 6 July, 1944, page 231)

4. What is your reaction to the Saturday, 15 July, 1944 entry (pages 233-237)? Why is it such a lengthy entry?

5. Why does Anne call herself a "little bundle of contradictions" (page 239)?

Pages 242-258 — Epilogue and Afterword

1.   Why is August 4, 1944 significant?

2.   What is the fate of the Annexers?

3.   How does Anne's diary come to be a book for us to read today?

4.   How is Anne Frank remembered?

14

The Book's Characters

Name	Relationship to Anne	Three Words to Describe	Appearance	Do You Know Anyone Similar?

Decision-Making Grid

Problem: Anne is irritated by Mrs. Van Daan. Anne finds Mrs. Van Daan offensive and unpleasant.

Directions: Help Anne to problem solve. Read the four suggested choices below and add two of your own. Look at the criteria questions across the top. Add another criterion question of your own. Rate each of the choices using the criteria questions. Answer "yes," "no," or "maybe."

Choices	Will the choice solve the problem?	Will the choice make Anne feel better?	Will the choice cause any other harm?	
1. Do nothing.				
2. Talk to Mrs. Van Daan alone.				
3. Write a letter to Mrs. Van Daan.				
4. Ask parents for help.				

Name_____

What is Unique About the Diary Writing Format?

Directions: Fill in the puzzle to crystallize your ideas on the diary format. Discuss with a partner and add to your answers.

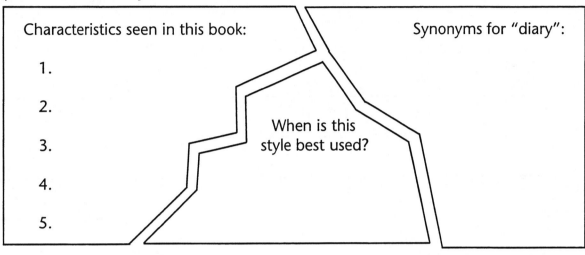

Characteristics seen in this book:

1.

2.

3.

4.

5.

Synonyms for "diary":

When is this style best used?

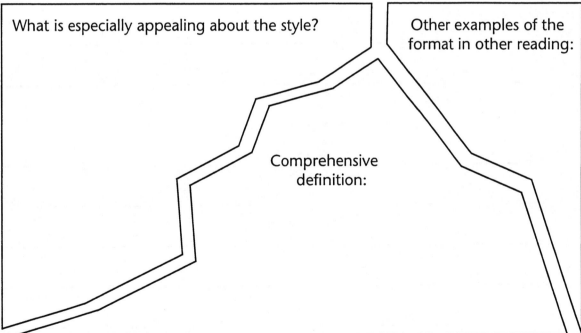

What is especially appealing about the style?

Other examples of the format in other reading:

Comprehensive definition:

Journal Writing — What is the Style?

Directions: Try writing in the style of the book. Choose a day in your life to use as the basis for your journal entry.

Dear _____,

_____

_____

_____

_____

_____

_____

_____

_____

_____

_____

_____

_____

_____

_____

Name_____

Anne Frank: The Diary of a Young Girl
Activity #11: Character Analysis / Higher Order Thinking
Use As Book Is Read After Introduction of Analogies

Anne Frank and Analogies

Directions: Drawing on your understanding of analogies (relationships), create some analogies using the character of Anne Frank as one of the elements.

For example:
Anne Frank : Pim   as   daughter : father

Anne Frank : _____   as   _____ : _____

Anne Frank : _____   as   _____ : _____

Anne Frank : _____   as   _____ : _____

Anne Frank : _____   as   _____ : _____

Anne Frank : _____   as   _____ : _____

Name_____

Anne, the Writer of the Diary

Directions: Read the listing of feeling words. Circle any feelings that apply to Anne Frank. Choose five words to use in sentences explaining when in the book the particular words would apply.

joy	annoyed	silly	understood	touched
hopeful	frightened	infuriated	bummed	uncertain
intimidated	carefree	bored	ecstatic	envious
disheartened	lonely	ashamed	jealous	childish
angry	guilty	melancholy	righteous	mad
embarrassed	hate	indignant	discouraged	tense
dislike	uncomfortable	frustrated	uptight	loved
anxious	irritated	comfortable	liked	burdened
appreciation	puzzled	sexy	cornered	wistful
confused	uninterested	getting even	gypped	disgusted
playful	revengeful	ripped off	revolted	regretful
competent	proud	self-conscious	left-out	abused
inadequate	ornery	rejected	distrustful	unloved
resentful	hurt	trusting	grateful	naughty
stumped	defeated	excited	crabby	lost
recognized	agitated	pressured	enthusiastic	important
nervous	afraid	empty	satisfied	dumb
scared	accepting	criticized	dissatisfied	support
energetic	fed up	bugged	persistent	stubborn
respect	judged	disappointed	glad	sad
pretty	witty	gay	odd	taken back
surprised	startled	rage	dirty	shame
loathing	sorrow	anguish	agony	dread
delight	humiliated	depleted	tired	used
outraged	upset	irritable	fury	passivity
sloth	weary	dreary	lazy	greed
contempt	good	light	alive	optimistic
relaxed	infatuated	hopeful	peaceful	involved
glad	admiration	ambition	happy	concern

Look back to the first entry of the book. Why does it provide a good beginning?

What connections are there between this book and your own life? Explain.

Consider the sharing of space in the room from Dussel's view-point. What would he write to Kitty?

What were your feelings after reading of the Franks going into hiding? After reading half the book? After finishing the book?

Why is the book so often included on suggested reading lists and in school units?

What are the hardest things about being fourteen? To expand your ideas on the subject, ask a few friends.

How would you spend your time if you couldn't move about freely and attend school?

How would the situation be different for the Secret Annexe folks in today's world?

A Book Review

Directions: Imagine a book review of the *Anne Frank: The Diary of a Young Girl* as it might have appeared in a Dutch newspaper shortly after it was published.

_____

_____

_____

_____

_____

_____

_____

_____

_____

_____

Comprehension Quiz

Directions: Mark T or F on the line to the left of each numbered statement.

____ 1. Anne Frank is a fifteen-year-old Jew living in Denmark at the start of the book.

____ 2. Kitty is Anne's pet cat.

____ 3. Anne and her family flee to Canada where they hide their true Jewish identities.

____ 4. The Franks voluntarily go into hiding when Anne's sister Margot receives a call-up notice.

____ 5. The Secret Annexe is behind the warehouse where Mr. Frank had worked.

____ 6. There are ten people hiding in the Secret Annexe—4 Franks, 4 Van Daans, and 2 Dussels.

____ 7. The Secret Annexe folks rely solely on information from Elli to learn of the outside world.

____ 8. Food for the Secret Annexe is left in the office.

____ 9. The Franks are thought in the community to have fled to Maastricht.

___ 10. Anne and her sister Margot pass their days sewing, knitting, and quilting.

___ 11. Mrs. Van Daan is a pleasant grandmotherly type who dotes on Anne.

___ 12. Anne is pleased that Peter Van Daan is in the Annexe because he was her friend since age five.

___ 13. Mr. Dussel is a dentist by trade.

___ 14. Anne writes daily in her diary, even if only a short entry.

___ 15. As the time together in the Secret Annexe grows, those living together bond and grow much friendlier with each other.

Directions: Choose two of the following words to use in a sentence, demonstrating your understanding:

lorries	het	Gestapo	barrage
camomile	clandestine	pedantic	procured

Comprehension Quiz

Directions: Mark T or F on the line to the left of each numbered statement.

___ 1. Mummy's first wish when allowed to go outside is for a cup of coffee.

___ 2. The good news on the radio in 1943 is that Mussolini has resigned, the Fascist party is banned, and Italy has surrendered to the Allies.

___ 3. Anne shares her bedroom in the Secret Annexe with her older sister Margot.

___ 4. Mrs. Van Daan always offers the best food and an ample portion to her husband and Pim.

___ 5. Elli is the Van Daan's cat.

___ 6. Potato peeling is a daily chore in the Secret Annexe, shared by all at various times.

___ 7. Mr. and Mrs. Van Daan decide to sell her jewelry to provide cash for the household expenses.

___ 8. Anne's fountain pen is found under the divan when the couch is moved for cleaning.

___ 9. Peter and Anne spend time talking in the attic room.

___ 10. Anne is fond of the name Peter because it was her favorite uncle's name.

___ 11. 1943 and 1944 are years of improving conditions for the Dutch people.

___ 12. Margot and Anne sort out their relationships with Peter and sibling competition by writing letters.

___ 13. The Franks are more demonstrative in their affection than the Van Daans.

___ 14. Those in the Secret Annexe do office work after hours, carrying typewriters up into the Annexe after others have gone home.

___ 15. Anne's diary provides not only a view of the hardships for Jews in Holland during World War II but also a chronicle of adolescence.

Unit Exam

Part I — Identification: Find a character on the right who matches the description on the left. Write the letter of the character next to the matching number. Each character may be used more than once or not at all.

_____ 1. Sells her fur coat

_____ 2. Frank's business partner

_____ 3. Pim

_____ 4. Dentist

_____ 5. Found Anne's diary

_____ 6. Survived concentration camps

_____ 7. Ambition to be a journalist

_____ 8. Hospitalized

_____ 9. Featured in Anne's dreams

_____ 10. Call-up caused Franks to go into hiding

_____ 11. Engaged

_____ 12. Van Daan pet

_____ 13. Link to outside world

_____ 14. Shares room with Anne

_____ 15. Exchanges letters with Anne

_____ 16. Born in Germany

_____ 17. Name given to Anne's diary

_____ 18. Sleeps in the attic

_____ 19. Argues loudly

_____ 20. Born to wealth

A. Anne Frank

B. Kitty

C. Mr. Koophuis

D. Mr. Kraler

E. Mr. Frank

F. Mr. Van Daan

G. Mrs. Van Daan

H. Peter Van Daan

I. Mrs. Frank

J. Margot Frank

K. Miep

L. Peter Wessel

M. Elli

N. Albert Dussel

O. Mouschi

Part II — Complete the attribute web to give a view of Anne Frank. Choose eight descriptions to place on the lines.

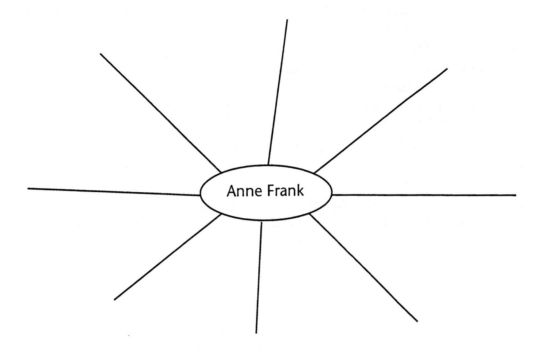

Choose one of your descriptions to expand into a short paragraph, including reasons for your choice of that description.

© Novel Units, Inc.

29

Part III: Put these events into chronological order:

A.   D-Day
B.   German invasion of Poland
C.   Franks flee to Holland from Germany.
D.   German forces overrun Belgium, Holland and France.
E.   Anne celebrates her fourteenth birthday.
F.   Franks go into hiding.
G.   Anne celebrates her thirteenth birthday.
H.   Anne enjoys Peter Van Daan.
I.   Anne celebrates her fifteenth birthday.
J.   The Franks' Secret Annexe is discovered and the occupants are sent to concentration camps.
K.   The Allies liberate Holland.
L.   Anne Frank dies.

1) _____   7) _____

2) _____   8) _____

3) _____   9) _____

4) _____   10) _____

5) _____   11) _____

6) _____   12) _____

Study Guide Suggested Answers

Introductory Pages
1. Translated from Dutch and copyright of 1952
2. Answers vary; "remarkable," "survival," "spirit."

Pages 1-56 — Sunday, 14 June, 1942 to Tuesday, 22 December, 1942
1. Calendar entries written to "Kitty," dates and entries chosen randomly.
2. Setting—Holland during WWII. Conflict—survival of Jewish "family" group in hiding. Characters—Franks, Van Daans, Dussel, those who assist them.
3. honest, forthright, inquisitive
4. Answers will vary.
5. Answers will vary.

Pages 57-79 — Wednesday, 13 January, 1943 to Tuesday, 13 July, 1943
1.

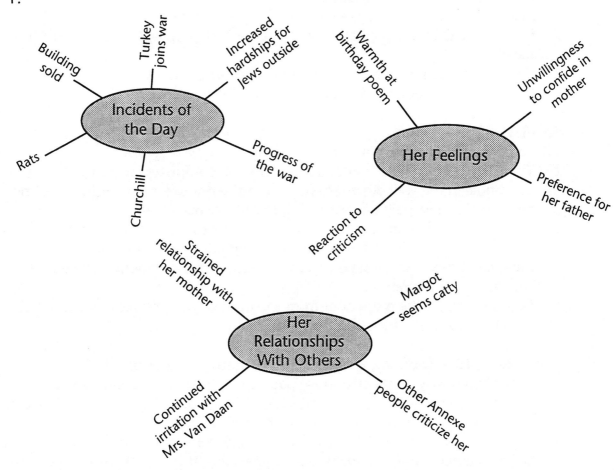

Pages 80-114 — Friday, 16 July, 1943 to Wednesday, 29 December, 1943

1. There is little difference in day-to-day life, although interpersonal relationships are more intense and the progress of the war is intensified as are hardships outside the Secret Annexe.
2. police action against them
3. burglars (page 80), air-raid (page 83), shooting at night (page 88), Koophuis is ill and hospitalized (pages 100-101), door bell ring (page 103), V. M. curiosity (page 98)
4. disagreements and criticism among the residents (e.g., pages 83-84), fleas from the cat (page 85), Dussel's sleeping habits (page 87), Van Daan row over lack of money (page 101), flu (page 109)

Pages 114-174 — Sunday, 2 January, 1944 to Friday, 31 March, 1944

1. Mother—She continues to question the depth of the love and wants more.
   Margot—After exchange of letters about Peter, they reach new understanding and recognition of love and affection.
   Peter—He becomes a boyfriend, companion, and confidante.
2. build-up to D-Day, anticipation, aftermath of fall of Italy, U.S. and Allied forces in Italy
3. a girlfriend, someone to share her adolescent thoughts and questions
4. She is more mature, less volatile, and more introspective.

Pages 174-205 — Saturday, 1 April, 1944 to Sunday morning, 7 May, 1944

1. To be a journalist; her diary writings suggest that it is an apt fit.
2. There is a burglary at the warehouse. The male Annexers scare the thieves away but a hole in the wall draws attention and the Annexers spend the weekend in fear and darkness lest police investigating might discover them.
3. toilet, unknown, inability to summon help, fear of discovery, nourishment
4. Her growing affection for Peter concerns her father who asks Peter and her to stop meeting in the attic. Anne is unhappy and asserts her independence in a letter which offends her father.
5. Security leaks, bolting the door from the inside. The Annexers enact stricter security measures on themselves.

Pages 205-241 — Monday, 8 May, 1944 to Tuesday, 1 August, 1944

1. Answers will vary. Anticipation — page 213; Despair — pages 216-217; Happiness — pages 210, 219-221, 223, 227; Hunger — page 216; Discomfort — pages 212, 218-219; Busyness — pages 209, 232.
2. D-Day; they anticipate the English invasion for a long time before it comes. When D-Day happens, they are much encouraged that they will be rescued and that the war will be over soon.

3. Religious beliefs and having goals and purposes in life provides the individual resolve and strength of character.
4. Answers vary; Anne is sorting herself out and defining herself after reading a book criticizing youth of today.
5. She is thoughtful and contemplative, able to see different views and aspects of an issue.

Epilogue and Afterword
1. It is the date that the Secret Annexe is discovered and the inhabitants as well as Kraler and Koophuis are sent to concentration camps.
2. All die except Mr. Frank, Kraler and Koophuis.
3. The Gestapo plunder the Secret Annexe but don't take the diary. Elli and Miep find it afterward and Mr. Frank authorizes publication and translation after the war.
4. Answers will vary.

Answer Key

In both comprehension quizzes, teachers may ask students to correct the false statements.

Comprehension Quiz Answers — After Page 79
1. F (she is thirteen in Holland)
2. F (name of her diary)
3. F (family goes into hiding in Amsterdam)
4. T
5. T
6. F (8 people—4 Franks, 3 Van Daans, 1 Dussel)
7. F (They have a radio.)
8. F (Food is left in warehouse.)
9. T
10. F (They read and study.)
11. F (Mrs. Van Daan, a cantankerous woman, is hard on Anne.)
12. F (Anne meets Peter when the families go into hiding.)
13. T
14. F (She writes intermittently.)
15. F (Time together strains relations among the Secret Annexe folks.)

Comprehension Quiz Answers — Pages 80-174
1. T
2. T
3. F (shares with Mr. Dussel)
4. F (Mrs. Van Daan is a bit greedy and takes larger portions and the best foods for herself.)
5. F (Elli works in the factory, runs errands for the Annexers, and often eats dinner with them.)
6. T
7. F (They sell her fur coat.)
8. F (The fountain pen is accidentally burned in the stove.)
9. T
10. F (An early infatuation was for a Peter Wessel.)
11. F (The conditions worsened.)
12. T
13. T
14. T
15. T

Exam Answers

Part I

1.	G	11.	M	
2.	C, D	12.	O	
3.	E	13.	C, D, K, M	
4.	N	14.	N	
5.	M, K	15.	J	
6.	C, D, E	16.	A, E, I, J	
7.	A	17.	B	
8.	C	18.	H	
9.	L	19.	F	
10.	J	20.	E, I, A, J	

Part II — See essay evaluation form on page 36.

Part III

1. C
2. B
3. D
4. G
5. F
6. E
7. H
8. A
9. I
10. J
11. L
12. K

Essay Evaluation Form

1. **Focus:** Student writes a clear thesis
   and includes it in the opening paragraph.   10   8   4

2. **Organization:** The final draft reflects
   the assigned outline; transitions are
   used to link ideas.   20   16   12

3. **Support:** Adequate quotes are provided
   and are properly documented.   12   10   7

4. **Detail:** Each quote is explained (as if
   the teacher had not read the book);
   ideas are not redundant.   12   10   7

5. **Mechanics:** Spelling, capitalization, and
   usage are correct.   16   12   8

6. **Sentence Structure:** The student avoids
   run-ons and sentence fragments.   10   8   4

7. **Verb:** All verbs are in the correct tense;
   sections in which plot is summarized are
   in the present tense.   10   8   4

8. Total effect of the essay.   10   8   4
   _____
                                                       100   80   50

Comments:

                                               Total: _____

(This rubric may be altered to fit the needs of a particular class. You may wish to show
it to students before they write their essays. They can use it as a self-evaluation tool,
and they will be aware of exactly how their essays will be graded.)